REBECCA FERGUSON

From Stage to Stardom – The Journey of a Versatile Talent"

Richard G. Ramirez

TABLE OF CONTENTS

INTRODUCTION

Among the many elements that make up the enormous constellation of Hollywood stars is Rebecca Ferguson. This icon, who was born in Stockholm, Sweden, has become well-known in the film industry thanks to her talent, tenacity, and enigmatic charm, which captivates audiences everywhere.

Ferguson's path started with her formative years spent in the quaint alleyways of Stockholm and advanced through a range of encounters and inspirations. She was always drawn to the performing and storytelling arts since she was raised in a home that valued creativity and promoted imagination. Her early commitment to the arts laid the foundation for a career that would ultimately establish her reputation in the annals of cinema history.

Ferguson's rise to prominence demonstrated her unrelenting commitment to her career. In every role she played, she infused her characters with nuance and authenticity, drawing viewers into the imaginary worlds she crafted. Ferguson's versatility and variety, showcased by her breakthrough performances in Swedish cinema and her quick ascent in Hollywood, have made her one of the most intriguing and sought-after talents of her generation.

Submerged beneath the glitz and glamour of the big screen, Ferguson's tale is one of perseverance and determination. Through the highs and lows of the entertainment industry, she has persisted in her pursuit of excellence, continuously pushing the boundaries of her creativity and challenging herself in each new job.

As we begin our analysis of Rebecca Ferguson's life and career, we are urged to delve deeply into her extraordinary journey, which is marked by passion, determination, and an unflinching dedication to the art of acting. With her mesmerizing performances and seductive appearance, Ferguson has cemented her place as one of the film industry's emerging stars and left a lasting impression.

CHAPTER 1: INTRODUCTION AND FORMATIVE YEARS:

Rebecca Ferguson's early life and upbringing helped to shape her into a captivating storyteller. She was born on October 19, 1983, in a multicultural and historically varied setting in Stockholm, Sweden. Her destiny as an actor and performer would continue to be shaped by her family.

Ferguson grew up in the busy Vasastan district of central Stockholm, where a range of factors influenced her development. Her parents, who were also in the arts, instilled in her a deep respect for artistic expression and creativity. Ferguson became engrossed in theater, music, and literature as a result of the city's varied dynamic.

Ferguson was reared in a caring environment, but she had a challenging childhood. When her parents divorced when she was a little child, her mother was the only one to raise her. However, it was during this chaotic period that Ferguson's resilience and resolve took hold, shaping her into the strong, independent woman she would eventually become.

While overcoming the difficulties of adolescence, Ferguson discovered a love for performing, which would eventually lead her to her future career. She participated in school plays and local theater performances, which helped her hone her skills and ignite her passion for acting. Ferguson had an eye-catching charisma and a natural talent that were apparent from an early age.

Ferguson chose to follow her dream after high school and enrolled at the esteemed Adolf Fredrik's Music School in Stockholm to concentrate on musical theater.During this early training phase, Ferguson acquired the techniques and abilities necessary to become an expert in her field, preparing her for the challenges and opportunities that were ahead.

Ferguson's early exposure to Swedish film helped her succeed when she joined the professional acting scene. Her ability to be adaptable and mature beyond her years in every character she played won her both professional recognition and critical acclaim.

We can learn about the experiences and forces that shaped Rebecca Ferguson into the talented actress she is today by following her life narrative. Ferguson's narrative is one of tenacity, passion, and unshakable commitment to her art, from her childhood in Stockholm to her foray into the performing profession.

1.1 Growing Up in Sweden:

Rebecca Ferguson's childhood in Sweden was woven together by her close family ties, the vibrant hues of Scandinavian culture, and the growth of her creative soul. Born in Stockholm on October 19, 1983, Ferguson grew up surrounded by her own country's colorful culture.

Growing up in the busy Vasastan area in the center of Stockholm, Ferguson was surrounded by the sights, sounds, and rhythms of city life. The multicultural ambiance of the Swedish capital provided a fertile ground for her growing imagination and voracious curiosity. Young Rebecca was promised exploration and excitement in every area of Stockholm, from its cobblestone alleys bordered by old buildings to its verdant parks.

Ferguson was raised in a caring, encouraging, and artistic household. Her parents, who were also artists, instilled in her a deep passion for literature, music, and theater. Ferguson was encouraged to advance her abilities and pursue her interests, and their home became a sanctuary for her artistic expression.

Ferguson came from a safe, loving home, but she had a rough upbringing. Her parent's divorce had left her early life chaotic and uncertain, so she had to learn early on how to handle the difficulties of family dynamics. But it was in these early years that Ferguson's moral fortitude and fortitude began to manifest, laying the foundation for the steadfast attitude that would define her later years.

Growing up in Sweden, Ferguson found solace and inspiration in the surrounding natural beauty. The scenery, which spanned from the expansive woodlands that crisscrossed the Swedish countryside to the serene waters of the Stockholm archipelago, provided comfort for her budding creative spirit.

Ferguson's enthusiasm for performing began to blossom as a result of her early hardships and successes. She discovered a passion for narrative and a talent for acting via impromptu performances with pals, school plays, and neighborhood theater troupes. During these early years, Ferguson's acting career began to take shape, setting the stage for the incredible voyage that lay ahead.

When we reflect on Rebecca Ferguson's formative years in Sweden, we see a reflection of the experiences and factors that shaped the resilient, intelligent, and compassionate adult she would eventually grow up to be. Her early years, which took her from the bustling streets of Stockholm to the tranquil countryside of Sweden, stood as a tribute to the transformational power of love, creativity, and the infinite capacity of the human soul.

1.2 Effects on Families:

The threads of Rebecca Ferguson's family's influence are intricately interwoven with her acting career; each member contributes a unique and noteworthy piece to the overall fabric of her life and career. Ferguson's family played a crucial role in shaping her values, nurturing her talents, and providing unwavering support for the entirety of her journey—from her formative years in Stockholm, Sweden, to her rise to international prominence.

The Ferguson family dynamic was based on a deep sense of love, kinship, and respect for one another. Ferguson's parents split, so she was raised by her mother and grandmother. From an early age, she learned the importance of perseverance and resilience. Ferguson's mother, a talented actress and director, provided guidance and inspiration as well as a deep understanding of the storytelling art and the impact of performance. Ferguson gained a lot of knowledge about the transformational potential of acting and how it can impact both performers and audiences by witnessing her mother's dedication to her craft and attending practices and performances.

Along with her family, Ferguson's extended family also had a wide range of influences that influenced her viewpoint and motivated her to achieve her goals. Ferguson's horizons and understanding of the world were broadened and enhanced by the diverse perspectives and experiences she encountered from her relatives who were employed in many creative industries, including music, writing, and the visual arts. Ferguson's family, whether through animated discussions at the dinner table or family-uniting group projects, fostered an environment of inquiry, discovery, and creative expression that nourished her passion for storytelling and performance.

Ferguson was raised with strong moral principles and ethics by her family, which served as a guide for her throughout her career, even outside of the arts. Ferguson was raised with honesty, sincerity, and compassion as values. She also discovered the importance of remaining true to who she is and inspiring people via her position. These core values provided her with a moral compass and a sense of direction that transcended the pursuit of fame and wealth, enabling her to successfully negotiate the highs and lows of the entertainment business.

As Ferguson's career climbs to new heights, her family is a continual source of love, support, and inspiration. From her modest beginnings in Stockholm to her achievements on the international stage, their steadfast support has been a constant source of inspiration for her, igniting her passion for storytelling and giving her the confidence to pursue her aspirations with unyielding tenacity and grace. Ferguson honors the relationships that have influenced her path as an actress and her family while celebrating the transformative power of love, connection, and shared ambitions.

1.3 The Beginning of a Formative Career:

Rebecca Ferguson's early career was marked by a combination of perseverance, courage, and unwavering devotion to her craft. Ferguson's life story, which begins with her humble origins in Stockholm, Sweden, and ends with her rise to recognition as one of Hollywood's most fascinating talents, is a monument to the transformative power of desire and tenacity.

Ferguson took her first serious steps into the acting industry when she joined the prestigious Adolf Fredrik's Music School in Stockholm during her early years to learn musical theater. As her skills improved, she discovered the subtleties of acting and immersed herself in the complex narrative. While learning under seasoned professors and working with other young actors, Ferguson developed a great love for theater and an aptitude for character acting. Her career in the performing arts was set in motion by this.

When Ferguson began her career as a professional actor, she encountered both challenges and achievements. She showed tenacity and resolve in her early years as she navigated the competitive entertainment industry, going through many auditions, getting turned down, and landing small roles in Swedish films. Ferguson overcame several challenges to achieve her ambitions, drawing strength from her unfailing support system in her family and her passion for her career.

Ferguson's career took off once she was cast in the breakthrough role of "Nya Tider," a Swedish soap opera, where she became well-known for her fascinating performance. After that, Ferguson's career took off. She was chosen for several highly renowned Swedish films and television shows, for which she won awards and garnered recognition for her versatility and subtle acting style.

However, Ferguson's relocation to Hollywood would be the catalyst for her global public recognition. She made her English-language debut as Elizabeth Woodville in the 2013 BBC drama "The White Queen," which highlighted her as a rising figure to watch. Filmmakers and casting directors were drawn to Ferguson's ground-breaking performance, which led to a plethora of career prospects in Hollywood.

Since then, Ferguson has captured the attention of audiences with a string of spectacular film and television roles. These include her crucial part in "Mission: Impossible – Rogue Nation" and her nuanced depiction of Jenny Lind in "The Greatest Showman." With each project Ferguson takes on, she continues to push the boundaries of her career and captivate viewers with her depth, tenderness, and all-around fascinating presence.

Rebecca Ferguson's modest beginnings in her profession serve as a reminder of the transformational power that comes from having passion, perseverance, and unflinching self-belief. Ferguson's story, which starts with humble origins in Stockholm and ends with her ascent to Hollywood celebrity, serves as an example for aspiring actresses worldwide and demonstrates the persistence of aspirations and the unflinching pursuit of perfection.

CHAPTER 2: ASCENT TO NOTORIETY:

Rebecca Ferguson's rise to prominence is evidence of her talent, her perseverance, and the power of a ground-breaking performance to transform an individual. Ferguson's journey, from her modest beginnings in Swedish cinema to her rise to international prominence, is an engaging narrative of persistence, willpower, and unwavering dedication to her work.

Ferguson first gained notoriety for her breakthrough role as Anna Gripenhielm in the Swedish soap opera "Nya Tider," for which she was praised for playing a believable and complex character. Following this initial triumph, Ferguson's career took off as she went on to play prominent parts in several well-regarded Swedish films and television shows, winning accolades for her acting abilities and critical acclaim.

Ferguson's transition to English-language cinema, however, would be the one that truly put her on the international map. Her riveting performance as Elizabeth Woodville in the BBC miniseries "The White Queen," which had its premiere in 2013, won over both fans and reviewers. Ferguson's rapid rise to popularity in

Hollywood was made possible by her critical praise and status as a rising star from her breakthrough performance in the series.

Following the success of "The White Queen," Ferguson's career took off, and she went on to star in some well-known movies, including "Hercules" and "Mission: Impossible – Rogue Nation." Ferguson's depiction of the enigmatic Ilsa Faust in the latter garnered critical acclaim, elevating her profile nationally and securing her position as one of Hollywood's most sought-after actors.

Ferguson got her big break in 2017 when she was cast as Jenny Lind in the musical biopic "The Greatest Showman." Her haunting rendition of "Never Enough" drew attention from admirers worldwide, garnering her critical acclaim and solidifying her status as a genuine star. The film's success catapulted Ferguson into the realm of Hollywood stardom and made her a highly sought-after and versatile actress in the industry.

Since then, Ferguson has captivated audiences with her alluring performances in a range of movies, such as historical dramas and action thrillers. Ferguson's captivating presence, which transcends the screen in every part she portrays, enthralls critics and fans alike.

Rebecca Ferguson's amazing rise to prominence serves as a reminder of the transformational power of talent, perseverance, and unflinching self-belief. Ferguson's story demonstrates the enduring fascination of the silver screen as well as the unwavering determination of those who dare to dream. It started with modest beginnings in Swedish cinema and concluded with her climb to international recognition.

2.1 The Pioneering Role:

In "Mission: Impossible – Rogue Nation" (2015), Rebecca Ferguson made her big screen debut as the alluring Ilsa Faust. Her career took a major shift after this performance, which solidified her status as a rising star in the industry.

Ferguson's character Ilsa Faust, from "Mission: Impossible – Rogue Nation," is an enigmatic and accomplished MI6 operative who gets entangled in a dangerous game of espionage. By demonstrating herself to be a powerful, multifaceted character who challenges the assumptions of both the audience and the main character, Ethan Hunt, Ilsa Faust defies clichés as a femme fatale with a dark history and sinister motivations.

Ferguson's performance of Ilsa Faust captured the attention of reviewers and audiences alike with its subtlety, profundity, and all-around compelling presence. Ferguson's steely will, perfect fighting technique, and enticing attractiveness gave the role a feeling of realism and complexity. These qualities enabled her to go beyond the cliché of the action heroine and made her a formidable presence in the movie business.

Ferguson's depiction of Ilsa Faust stands out because of her ability to give the character layers of depth and emotion, showing flashes of inner anguish and competing loyalties beneath her icy façade. Ferguson brought a human element and relatability to Ilsa Faust, which made it easier for audiences to empathize with her throughout both quiet and intense action sequences.

Ferguson's rapport with co-star Tom Cruise, who plays Ethan Hunt, improved her performance even more. Viewers throughout the world were captivated by their dynamic and fascinating on-screen connection. Their enduring connection and mutual respect added complexity to the film's plot, elevating the whole experience and leaving a lasting impression on audiences.

Rebecca Ferguson's breakthrough performance came in "Mission: Impossible – Rogue Nation," which thrust her into the public eye and garnered her widespread praise for her acting prowess. With her compelling depiction of Ilsa Faust, Ferguson established herself as a rising star in the industry and proved that she could compete with Hollywood's biggest actresses.

Following her breakthrough performance in "Mission: Impossible – Rogue Nation," Ferguson's career took off, mostly due to several high-profile assignments that brought her breadth and skill as an actress to light. But fans will never forget her legendary portrayal of Ilsa Faust, which speaks to the transforming power of talent, perseverance, and steadfast self-belief.

2.2 Accolades from Opponents:

The climb to critical recognition that Rebecca Ferguson has experienced is proof of her tremendous talent, versatility, and ability to give her all to every part that she plays. From her early successes in Swedish cinema to her breakthrough roles in Hollywood, critics have praised Ferguson's nuanced performances and captivating representations.

Ferguson's portrayal of Anna Gripenhielm in the Swedish soap opera "Nya Tider" brought her initial taste of critical praise.Her performance in the show garnered praise from critics and audiences alike for its authenticity and subtlety. This early notoriety helped Ferguson's career take off, making it simpler for her to transition to English-language film and ultimately become a global celebrity.

However, Ferguson gained widespread recognition and rave reviews for her breakout role as Ilsa Faust in "Mission: Impossible – Rogue Nation" (2015). Ferguson's portrayal of the enigmatic MI6 spy won plaudits from critics who saw that she brought humanity, nuance, and complexity to the role. Ferguson was honored for her ability to break stereotypes and subvert expectations with her portrayal of Ilsa Faust, which challenged preconceived notions of the action heroine.

With the success of "Mission: Impossible – Rogue Nation," Ferguson's fascinating appearances in a range of productions won over critics once more. She received great acclaim for her haunting rendition of "Never Enough" in "The Greatest Showman" (2017), which also showcased her range as an actress and her vocal ability. Critics praised Ferguson's on-screen portrayal of the well-known opera soprano Jenny Lind for her ability to capture the spirit of the role with grace and realism.

Ferguson's reputation as a gifted and versatile actor was further solidified by her parts in films such as "Life" (2017), "Florence Foster Jenkins" (2016), and "Doctor Sleep" (2019). Critics praised Ferguson for her ability to portray a wide range of characters with nuance, complexity, and sincerity, showcasing her versatility in dramatic and genre roles.

In addition to her accomplishments in movies, critics have praised Ferguson for her work in television shows such as "The White Queen" (2013) and "The Handmaid's Tale" (2017–present). Her portrayal of Elizabeth Woodville in "The White Queen" won her widespread acclaim for her commanding performance and captivating presence, while her portrayal of Serena Joy

Waterford in "The Handmaid's Tale" showcased her ability to portray complex, morally ambiguous characters with nuance and depth.

Rebecca Ferguson's remarkable talent and fascinating performances have led her from critical praise to an enduring impact on the cinema business. On-screen, she never fails to enchant spectators. Ferguson consistently gains the respect and admiration of both critics and fans by demonstrating her brilliance and versatility in every character she plays, making her one of Hollywood's most gifted and versatile actors.

2.3 Acknowledgment Abroad:

Rebecca Ferguson's unquestionable talent, versatility, and alluring on-screen character all contributed to her climb to global renown. People throughout the world have respected and appreciated Ferguson for her achievements, which range from her breakthrough role in a Swedish film to her ascent to prominence in Hollywood.

Ferguson first gained widespread notice for her outstanding portrayal of Ilsa Faust in "Mission: Impossible – Rogue Nation" (2015). Ferguson played a complicated and enigmatic MI6 agent, captivating audiences with her steely willpower, perfect combat abilities, and irresistible beauty. Her portrayal of Ilsa Faust struck a chord with audiences worldwide, and she was praised and acknowledged for her ability to dominate the screen with grace and authenticity.

Ferguson's career took off after the success of "Mission: Impossible – Rogue Nation," as she was chosen for many prominent roles that showcased her range and acting prowess. Her depressing rendition of "Never

Enough" in "The Greatest Showman" (2017) captured the attention of audiences worldwide, winning her praise from critics and solidifying her status as a genuine star. Ferguson's profile was enhanced among a global audience as a result of the film's tremendous popularity, which increased her prominence and influence in the entertainment industry.

Ferguson's roles in films including "Doctor Sleep" (2019), "Life" (2017), and "Florence Foster Jenkins" (2016) further cemented her reputation as a global celebrity. Her ability to portray a wide range of characters with authenticity, depth, and nuance among audiences from different languages and cultures won her praise and recognition from critics as well as fans.

In addition to her work in movies, Ferguson has received recognition from all around the world for her roles in television series such as "The Handmaid's Tale" (2017–present) and "The White Queen" (2013). Her portrayal of complex, morally dubious characters in these shows captivated audiences around the globe, earning her critical acclaim and solidifying her position as one of Hollywood's most talented and versatile actors.

Rebecca Ferguson's ascent to international recognition is a testament to her remarkable ability, dedication, and enduring impact on the entertainment sector. Her attractive appearance and compelling performances on screen never fail to captivate audiences. Ferguson continues to establish herself as a global celebrity, gaining the respect and admiration of people from all walks of life with each new project.

CHAPTER 3: REMARKABLE ROLES IN FILM AND TELEVISION:

Rebecca Ferguson's career has been studded with numerous notable performances in both cinema and television, all of which highlight her tremendous talent, range, and ability to inhabit characters with depth and sincerity. From her breakthrough performances in Swedish cinema to her ascent to fame in Hollywood, Ferguson has left a lasting mark on the entertainment world with her fascinating representations and captivating presence on screen.

Ferguson's most well-known role to date was Ilsa Faust in "Mission: Impossible – Rogue Nation" (2015). Ferguson was a complicated and enigmatic MI6 agent, captivating spectators with her unwavering allure, steely drive, and faultless combat skills. Ferguson's performance of Ilsa Faust, which defied expectations and solidified her status as an action heroine worth seeing, won her a lot of accolades.

"The Greatest Showman" (2017) featured Ferguson in a stunning performance as the well-known opera soprano Jenny Lind. Performing "Never Enough" in a spooky manner, she captivated audiences worldwide with her singing talent and acting versatility. Ferguson's depiction of Jenny Lind garnered her praise from critics and enhanced her standing as a gifted and versatile singer.

Ferguson portrays Katharine Gun in "Official Secrets" (2019), which is another notable performance. Ferguson, who portrayed a real-life whistleblower who disclosed classified information about the government, impressed both audiences and reviewers with her powerful and nuanced portrayal. She received praise from critics for her portrayal of Katharine Gun, proving that she was capable of bringing depth and realism to characters who were ethically complex and nuanced.

Ferguson is well-known for her work in television as well as films. She has acted in programs such as "The Handmaid's Tale" (2017–present) and "The White Queen" (2013). Ferguson portrayed England's title queen, Elizabeth Woodville, in "The White Queen," displaying a commanding presence and powerful acting. For the part, she garnered a lot of accolades, solidifying her status as a rising talent to keep an eye on.

Ferguson performed admirably in "The Handmaid's Tale," portraying the complex and ethically murky Serena Joy Waterford. Critics praised her portrayal as Serena Joy, highlighting her nuanced and complicated ability to navigate the intricate relationships between control, power, and atonement.

Rebecca Ferguson's remarkable abilities, versatility, and enduring impact on the entertainment business are demonstrated by her notable roles in both film and television. Her engaging performances and enticing on-screen persona never fail to enthrall fans. With each new role she takes on, Ferguson demonstrates her talent and versatility as one of Hollywood's most respected and versatile actors, garnering the respect and adoration of audiences worldwide.

3.1 Role Analysis: [TV Show or Movie Title]

First, let's discuss Rebecca Ferguson's performance as the well-known opera singer and "Swedish Nightingale," Jenny Lind, in the 2017 motion picture "The Greatest Showman." In this role study, we'll discuss Ferguson's performance, personal development, and impact on the film:

1. Character Overview: Jenny Lind is portrayed as a well-known opera soprano with a stunning voice and captivating stage presence. P.T. Barnum, played by Hugh Jackman, approaches her about touring America with his circus. Lind is shown as a sophisticated, beautiful, enigmatic individual with a strong moral compass and a strong feeling of artistic passion.

2. Performance: Rebecca Ferguson portrays Jenny Lind in a way that is both engaging and breathtakingly beautiful. Despite spending little time on screen, Ferguson captures the attention of viewers with her elegance, composure, and strong voice. Her performance in "Never Enough" is one of the film's highlights, showcasing her remarkable acting prowess and emotional spectrum.

3. Character Development: Despite Jenny Lind's initial dazzling and ethereal appearance, Ferguson gives the character layers of nuance and vulnerability. As the story goes on, we get to see glimpses of Lind's internal conflict and conflicting emotions, particularly in her interactions with P.T. Barnum. Ferguson's portrayal helps us relate to Lind's struggles and aspirations, which lends the character greater depth and dimension.

4. Effect on the Film: "The Greatest Showman" gains greater depth and poignancy from Rebecca Ferguson's portrayal of Jenny Lind. Her role sets the stage for the film's exploration of fame, ambition, and the search for happiness. Ferguson's portrayal elevates the film's ideas and narrative, leaving an impression on spectators long after the credits have rolled.

Lastly, Rebecca Ferguson's performance as Jenny Lind in "The Greatest Showman" exemplifies her exceptional acting talent and versatility. Ferguson's captivating portrayal, which offers the character depth, nuance, and emotional resonance, has a lasting imprint on the film and garners great praise from critics and audiences alike.

3.2 Character Development:

Let's look at Rebecca Ferguson's development as Ilsa Faust in "Mission: Impossible – Rogue Nation" (2015):

1. Introduction: An intriguing and mysterious MI6 agent with a questionable past is introduced as Illusa Faust. She is introduced to us as a crafty and intelligent operator who operates in total secrecy from the moment she first meets Tom Cruise's character Ethan Hunt, a.k.a. Faust.
2. Establishing Traits: Faust is initially presented as a morally problematic character who works in the shadowy fields of espionage and intelligence gathering. Her readiness to betray both allies and rivals to further her aims has created a climate of suspicion and anxiety among the other members of the IMF team.

3. Complexity and Vulnerability: As the story goes on, we catch glimpses of Faust's internal conflict and allegiance betrayals. Despite putting up a stoic façade, she is troubled by the consequences of her choices and the toll they have taken on her conscience. She regrets and questions her previous decisions as well.

4. Relationship Dynamics: A key aspect of Faust's character development is the way her relationship with

Ethan Hunt changes over time. Their encounters are marked by tension and distrust at first as they dance a fine line between treachery and trust. However, as the story progresses, we see how their bond develops and changes as they come to respect and admire each other's virtues, shortcomings, and skills.

5. atonement and Growth: Throughout the film, Faust sets out on a journey of self-discovery and atonement as she confronts her past and strives to atone for her actions. Her relationship with Ethan Hunt and the IMF team catalyzes her metamorphosis as she learns to trust others and values her morality and integrity.

6. Resolution: By the time the film ends, Faust has changed, becoming a new person who is committed to a different path and has been saved by her actions. Her capacity to shift from a morally problematic and conflicted agent to a trustworthy ally and friend is proof of her resilience and adaptability.

The character development that Rebecca Ferguson brought to Ilsa Faust in "Mission: Impossible – Rogue Nation" is a masterclass. Ferguson's subtle portrayal, which gives the character depth, complexity, and emotional resonance, defies the conventions of the action heroine role and makes Faust one of the most intriguing and unforgettable characters in Hollywood history.

3.3 Insights from Behind the Scenes:

Behind-the-scenes glimpses inside Rebecca Ferguson's "Mission: Impossible – Rogue Nation" (2015) performance demonstrate her dedication, flexibility, and collaborative attitude as an actress.

1. Physical Training: To prepare for her part as the astute and capable MI6 agent Ilsa Faust, Ferguson underwent a demanding physical training regimen. She immersed herself in martial arts, stunt work, and weapons training to convincingly capture the character's combat skill and agility. Ferguson shows in the behind-the-scenes film that she is committed to overcoming the physical difficulties of the role by performing her stunts with expertise and intensity.

2. Dynamic chemistry with Tom Cruise: Ferguson's portrayal of Ethan Hunt in "Mission: Impossible – Rogue Nation" is significantly impacted by her lively friendship with Cruise. Behind the scenes, their connection and chemistry are evident as they collaborate closely to add depth and authenticity to their on-screen partnership. Ferguson highlights the tight bond between the two actors by praising Cruise's dedication and

professionalism in interviews and behind-the-scenes recordings.

3. Character Preparation: Ferguson went into Ilsa Faust's past, motivations, and emotional journey in great detail. Ferguson discusses how she prepares characters behind the scenes, emphasizing the need for empathy and vulnerability in bringing Faust to life. She collaborated extensively with filmmaker Christopher McQuarrie and the film's creative team to ensure that Faust's arc was realistic and emotionally stirring.

4. Costume and Makeup: The costume and makeup teams played a major role in Ferguson's transition into the glamorous and enigmatic Ilsa Faust. A behind-the-scenes film showcases the intricate costume design and makeup expertise that went into creating the classic look of Faust.

from stylish black attire to subtle yet striking makeup choices. Ferguson's transition into the part demonstrates the skill and artistic vision of the production crew.

5. On-Set Dynamics: Ferguson's professionalism and positive outlook made a big difference in the supportive and cooperative atmosphere on set. Behind-the-scenes tales demonstrate how Ferguson's kind disposition and openness to collaborate with her co-stars and crew

members promoted mutual respect and a sense of unity throughout the entire project.

Ultimately, behind-the-scenes glimpses into Rebecca Ferguson's "Mission: Impossible – Rogue Nation" part offer insight into her dedication, versatility, and cooperative nature as an actress. Ferguson's commitment to her work is seen in every facet of her performance, from her rigorous physical preparation to her thorough character development. This contributed to the film's success and solidified Ferguson's status as one of Hollywood's most fascinating actors.

CHAPTER 4: PERSONAL LIFE:

Rebecca Ferguson's private life is characterized by warmth, solitude, and a strong sense of commitment to her family and career. Despite her modest lifestyle, peeks inside her private life shed light on the experiences and principles that have influenced both the woman and the actor.

1. Family and Upbringing: Ferguson grew up in her native Sweden, which boasts a thriving cultural scene. October 19, 1983, was her birthdate in Stockholm. Following her parents' divorce, Ferguson was raised by her mother and grandmother, where she learned the importance of resilience, independence, and creativity at a young age. Her family's encouragement and support helped her develop a passion for the arts and laid the foundation for her acting career.

2. Education and Early Career: Ferguson started her performing career at the prestigious Adolf Fredrik's Music School in Stockholm, where she acquired her formal training in musical theater. Ferguson used this critical educational period to gain the techniques and abilities necessary to hone her profession and prepare for a career in the performing arts. Ferguson began her

career in Swedish cinema after graduating, landing roles in many highly regarded films and TV shows that showcased her versatility and acting prowess.

3. Ascent to Fame: Ferguson's breakout role as Ilsa Faust in "Mission: Impossible – Rogue Nation" (2015) signaled the start of her rise to international acclaim. She received a lot of praise and gained notoriety for her fascinating performance in the movie. Since then, Ferguson has made a name for herself as one of Hollywood's most in-demand actors by enthralling viewers with her compelling roles in a variety of productions.

4. Personal Beliefs and Values: Throughout her career, Ferguson has maintained her honesty, empathy, and genuineness as guiding principles. She gives every role she plays her all, bringing nuance and depth to her performances as she devotes her entire being to her characters. Outside of the spotlight, Ferguson is well known for her modest demeanor, laid-back style, and genuine appreciation for her teammates and supporters.

5. Privacy: Despite her success in the spotlight, Ferguson maintains a pretty quiet life, keeping details about her relationships and family out of the public eye. Striking a healthy balance between her personal and professional

lives, she loves her privacy and her relationships with the people who matter most to her.

In conclusion, Rebecca Ferguson's personal life is a reflection of her values, experiences, and dedication to her career. Throughout her life, from her Swedish childhood to her rise to international renown, Ferguson has shown resilience, authenticity, and a strong commitment to storytelling. Though she doesn't want to draw attention to herself, peeks inside her personal life reveal who she is: a strong, loving mother, and talented actress who never fails to captivate viewers with her mesmerizing on-screen personas.

4.1 Families and Interpersonal Bonds:

As a celebrated actress, Rebecca Ferguson maintains a balance between her personal and professional lives, which is evident in her relationships and family life. Even though she tends to keep private information private, the following observations on her relationships and family dynamics provide some insight into her world:

1. Parental Influence: Ferguson was raised in Stockholm, Sweden, and was greatly influenced by her mother and grandmother. Ferguson was blessed with a creative and supportive upbringing, and her family had a significant role in igniting her early passion for the arts. Ferguson's mother, who was employed in the arts, inspired her to have a deep appreciation for narrative, theater, and performance.

2. Motherhood: In 2018, Ferguson gave birth to a daughter, whom she prefers to keep quiet. Motherhood has undoubtedly had a significant impact on Ferguson's life, affecting her priorities and perspective. In interviews, Ferguson has expressed her affection for her child and her enjoyment of the perks and tribulations of

parenthood—all the while maintaining her ferocious privacy protections.

3. love Relationships: Ferguson has mostly kept details about her love relationships private because she has decided to be discreet about her personal life. Ferguson's love life has been the subject of speculation and innuendo, but she has never recognized any romantic relationships in public. She would want to focus on her career and family instead of drawing attention to her romantic relationships.

4. Family Support: Throughout her career, Ferguson has continuously expressed gratitude to her family for their unfailing support and encouragement, both emotionally and professionally. Their love and support have been a source of inspiration and strength for Ferguson, enabling her to follow her aspirations and handle the highs and lows of the entertainment industry with grace and resiliency.

Even though Rebecca Ferguson maintains the specifics of her personal connections and family life a secret, glimpses into her life provide insight into the strong values and foundations that have molded her into the person she is today. From her wonderful upbringing in Sweden to her journey into motherhood, Ferguson's connections and family dynamics highlight the importance of love, connection, and the continuing effect of those closest to her.

4.2 Balancing Personal and Work Life:

It takes a delicate dance for Rebecca Ferguson to find a balance between her demanding acting job and her desire to treasure her time with her family and friends. Here is a closer examination of Ferguson's method for achieving this equilibrium:

1. Prioritizing Family Time: Despite her busy schedule, Ferguson takes time for her family, especially her daughter. She treasures these moments as opportunities to unwind, revitalize, and fortify her bonds with her loved ones away from the spotlight of Hollywood. Whether she's spending a quiet weekend at home or going on outdoor adventures with her significant other, Ferguson appreciates and enjoys these moments.

2. Setting Boundaries: Ferguson purposefully sets boundaries to protect her time in a job where work schedules are notoriously rigid and hours vary greatly. When she's not working, she tries to maintain a good balance between her personal and professional obligations by finding time for herself and her loved ones. Ferguson establishes limits and priorities that help her balance the demands of her career with the needs of her relationships.

3. Embracing Flexibility: Ferguson believes that to reconcile her personal and professional life, flexibility is crucial. She understands that unforeseen opportunities and challenges may arise in both domains, requiring her to adapt and change as needed. Ferguson embraces flexibility and maintains an open mind to new experiences, which help her handle the ups and downs of her career and personal obligations with grace and resilience.

4. Seeking Support: Ferguson is aware of the need to have a strong support system to help her navigate the rigors of her personal and work life. Ferguson understands that she may get guidance and support from friends, family, and trustworthy coworkers to overcome life's challenges. Ferguson can surround herself with supportive and empowering people to help her overcome adversity and find bravery and comfort.

5. Practicing Self-Care: Ferguson includes self-care into her daily regimen as a way to rejuvenate and recharge in the face of her demanding schedule. To maintain balance and well-being in her life, Ferguson places great importance on taking care of herself. This involves engaging in mindfulness exercises, working out, and taking part in her favorite activities. If Ferguson takes time to look for her body, mind, and soul, she will be

able to handle the demands of her job and her relationships with greater skill.

Rebecca Ferguson's ability to balance her personal and professional lives demonstrates her perseverance, persistence, and determination to live a happy and meaningful life. Ferguson prioritizes spending time with her family, sets limits, accepts flexibility, asks for help when needed, and takes care of herself elegantly and genuinely to manage the challenges of her dual duties. She urges others to follow in her footsteps professionally.

4.3 Interests and Hobbies:

Rebecca Ferguson's hobbies and interests shed light on her many interests outside of acting and her nuanced nature. Ferguson manages to balance her busy schedule with interests that bring her satisfaction, fulfillment, and a sense of balance:

1. Outdoor Adventures: Ferguson has a deep reverence for nature and enjoys spending as much time outside as possible. Taking leisurely walks in the great outdoors, hiking along attractive routes, or visiting picturesque scenery are some of Ferguson's favorite ways to unwind and rejuvenate. Her passion for the outdoors gives her the inspiration and refreshment she needs to get through the turmoil of her busy life.

2. Travel & Exploration: Ferguson is an experienced tourist who enjoys experiencing different foods, customs, and cultures around the world. Ferguson sees traveling as a means of broadening her experiences, developing her viewpoint, and creating priceless memories with her loved ones. She likes to take spontaneous road trips and explore vibrant cities. She explores new locations and embarks on life-altering

adventures because of her curiosity and sense of adventure.

3. Literature and Reading: Ferguson is an avid reader who loves to read. She takes advantage of every chance to cozy up with a good book. Whether it's fiction, non-fiction, or poetry, reading provides Ferguson with both inspiration and enrichment. She immerses herself in narratives, ideas, and points of view that resonate with her. Her passion for reading stimulates her mind and inspires her creativity, which improves her understanding of the world and satisfies her imagination.

4. Music and the Performing Arts: Having studied musical theater, Ferguson has a deep respect for music and the performing arts.
When her schedule allows, she enjoys attending live events like theater shows and concerts, where she can lose herself in the story and the magic of music. Ferguson's love of music, which also brings her joy and inspiration, fuels her passion for the arts and her creative spirit.

5. Culinary Exploration: Ferguson is a foodie who loves to discover new flavors, cuisines, and cooking methods. Whether she's making new recipes at home, traveling to new places and sampling local specialties, or taking them to her favorite restaurants, Ferguson relishes the

sensations of food and the shared experience of dining. Her culinary adventures allow her to indulge her palate, expand her culinary horizons, and enjoy life's little joys.

Rebecca Ferguson's hobbies and interests are a reflection of her exuberance, spirit of exploration, and love of life. Whether she is traveling to new places, experiencing exciting cuisine, or spending time in nature, Ferguson finds inspiration, joy, and fulfillment in the diversity of experiences life has to offer.

CHAPTER 5: PHILANTHROPY AND ADVOCACY:

Rebecca Ferguson's advocacy activities and charity donations demonstrate her commitment to making a difference in the world and advancing the causes that she believes in. Ferguson is renowned for maintaining a quiet profile when it comes to her charity endeavors, but her backing of numerous initiatives and institutions demonstrates her dedication to giving back:

1. Humanitarian Causes: Ferguson is an enthusiastic advocate for causes that benefit internally displaced individuals, refugees, and marginalized communities around the globe. Through her support of organizations like Save the Children, UNICEF, and the United Nations Refugee Agency (UNHCR), she has spoken out in favor of the rights and well-being of children and families affected by violence, poverty, and displacement.

2. Women's Rights and Empowerment: Ferguson is a fervent supporter of women's access to reproductive health, gender equality, and education. She has supported organizations including the Malala Fund, Plan International, and the Global Fund for Women in her

advocacy for policies that promote the advancement and empowerment of women and girls around the world.

3. Environmental Conservation: Ferguson is passionate about environmental sustainability and conservation and is a big supporter of programs aimed at protecting the environment for future generations. She offers assistance to organizations like the World Wildlife Fund (WWF), Greenpeace, and the Sierra Club that strive to advance environmentally conscious policies and practices and increase public awareness of environmental problems.

4. Mental Health Awareness: Ferguson is a strong advocate for initiatives that improve mental health and the availability of mental health services. She is an outspoken supporter of de-stigmatizing mental health and has shared candid insights on her own experiences. She has worked in partnership with organizations such as Mind, the Mental Health Foundation, and NAMI (National Alliance on Mental Illness) to advance increased awareness, resources, and assistance for individuals coping with mental health concerns.

5. Arts Education and Access: Ferguson, who is a strong advocate for the arts, supports initiatives that improve arts accessibility and education for underserved groups. She has collaborated with organizations including Arts for All, the Young Storytellers Foundation, and the Boys

& Girls Clubs of America that support initiatives that allow children and youth to explore their creativity and express themselves via the arts.

Rebecca Ferguson's activism and philanthropic pursuits demonstrate her commitment to making a difference in the world and using her position for social good. Ferguson's dedication to giving back is a powerful reminder of the impact that one person can have when they lend their voices and support to causes that matter. This is evident in her support of women's rights advocacy, mental health awareness campaigns, environmental conservation efforts, and the advancement of arts education and access.

5.1 The Causes Supported by Rebecca Ferguson:

Rebecca Ferguson is a devoted advocate for numerous causes, lending her time, voice, and support to organizations that address a range of social, environmental, and humanitarian issues. Rebecca Ferguson is an advocate for the causes listed below:

1. Children's Rights and Well-Being: Ferguson is a fierce advocate for children's rights and well-being, having backed UNICEF, Save the Children, and the Malala Fund, among other groups. She is in favor of initiatives that give children access to safety, healthcare, and education everywhere, particularly those affected by violence, poverty, and displacement.

2. Refugee and Humanitarian Assistance: As part of its steadfast dedication to supporting refugees and internally displaced individuals, Ferguson works with organizations such as the International Rescue Committee (IRC), Mercy Corps, and the United Nations Refugee Agency (UNHCR). She advocates for policies and programs that raise awareness of the plight of refugees while providing assistance, security, and support to those who have been displaced.

3. Women's Rights and Empowerment: Ferguson is a vocal proponent of gender equality and women's empowerment and a fervent supporter of organizations like Plan International, Women for Women International, and the Global Fund for Women. She is in favor of initiatives that promote women's rights, economic empowerment, and equitable access to healthcare, education, and reproductive resources for girls and women worldwide.

4. Environmental Conservation: Ferguson is passionate about sustainability and environmental conservation, which is why he supports organizations like the World Wildlife Fund (WWF), Greenpeace, and the Sierra Club. She works to raise public awareness of environmental concerns like deforestation, climate change, and wildlife protection. She supports policies and practices that protect the environment for future generations.

5. Mental Health understanding: Ferguson is a strong advocate for groups working to de-stigmatize and increase public understanding of mental health concerns, such as Mind, the Mental Health Foundation, and NAMI (National Alliance on Mental Illness). She advocates for increased awareness, support, and services for people who are coping with mental illness by being transparent about her own experiences with mental health concerns.

6. Arts Education and Access: Ferguson, a passionate advocate for the arts, works with organizations such as the Boys & Girls Clubs of America, Arts for All, and the Young Storytellers Foundation to promote initiatives that improve underprivileged communities' access to and understanding of the arts. She is in favor of programs that allow children and teenagers to develop their creativity and express themselves artistically.

Rebecca Ferguson demonstrates her genuine desire to make a difference in the world and use her position for social good by her broad support of a wide range of organizations. Ferguson serves as a potent reminder of the importance of empathy, compassion, and cooperation in creating a more fair and just society. Her advocacy for women's empowerment, children's rights, refugee support, environmental conservation awareness, mental health awareness, and arts education and access demonstrates her dedication to these causes.

5.2 Contributions and Volunteering:

Through her humanitarian initiatives and services, Rebecca Ferguson embodies her unwavering passion for supporting marginalized groups and causes that hold personal significance for her. Ferguson likes to keep a quiet profile when it comes to her charity pursuits, but her involvement in many groups and initiatives shows her devotion to making a positive impact. An extensive rundown of some of her accomplishments and philanthropic activities is provided below:

1. Fundraising Events: Ferguson frequently participates in NGOs' campaigns and fundraising events to raise money and exposure for deserving causes. Ferguson participates in benefit performances, auctions, and galas as a volunteer, giving her time and assistance to help raise funds and resources for good causes.

2. Public Advocacy: Ferguson utilizes her platform to advocate for causes that are important to her, such as women's empowerment, mental health awareness, refugee help, children's rights, and environmental preservation. Through interviews, social media posts, and public appearances, Ferguson raises the voices of

disadvantaged communities, enabling individuals to participate in the process of changing the world.

3. Donations: Ferguson freely contributes her time, resources, and cash to charitable organizations that align with her values and interests. Ferguson would want to keep the details of her gifts confidential, but the groups she supports that address pressing social, environmental, and humanitarian issues have benefited greatly from her assistance.

4. Volunteer Work: In addition to her financial donations, Ferguson lends her time and experience to help philanthropic groups and initiatives. Ferguson actively engages in practical volunteer work to make a good difference in the lives of others. This work might take the form of community service initiatives, youth mentoring, or aiding refugees and internally displaced individuals.

5. Collaborations and Advocacy Campaigns: Ferguson advances the goals of philanthropic organizations and advocacy groups by working with them. Ferguson is involved in relationships that promote good change and social effects. She does this by participating in advocacy activities, offering her voice to public awareness campaigns, and serving as a spokesperson for important issues.

Rebecca Ferguson's altruistic pursuits and contributions reveal her unwavering commitment to improving the world and using her position for social good. Ferguson's involvement in fundraising events, public advocacy, donations, volunteer work, charity organizations, and partnerships all show her genuine concern for people and her dedication to creating a more just, egalitarian, and compassionate society for everyone.

5.3 Effect on Concerns of Society:

Rebecca Ferguson has a broad impact on social issues through her advocacy, philanthropic contributions, and the powerful themes she conveys in her acting roles. Through her platform, Ferguson has tackled a wide range of social concerns, promoting action on important causes, igniting discussion, and raising awareness. This is a detailed analysis of her impact on several societal issues:

1. Women's Rights and Empowerment: Ferguson is a fervent advocate for women's rights and empowerment. She has used her platform to raise awareness of issues including workplace discrimination, gender-based violence, and the lack of access to healthcare and education for women and girls. Ferguson has played powerful, multifaceted female roles in movies and television that reject stereotypes and inspire people to value their agency and autonomy.

2. Refugee Assistance and Humanitarian Aid: Ferguson is committed to providing aid to refugees and internally displaced individuals, raising awareness of their plight, and advocating for policies and programs that protect, shield, and assist marginalized communities. Through

her participation with organizations like Save the Children and UNHCR, Ferguson elevates the voices of refugees and encourages empathy and understanding for those who are forced to escape their homes due to conflict, persecution, and violence.

3. Destigmatization and Mental Health Awareness: Ferguson is a strong advocate for these causes, sharing personal tales and discussing the importance of eradicating the stigma associated with mental illness. Ferguson promotes open communication by standing out for reform and endorsing organizations like Mind and NAMI. access to services and help for those with mental health concerns.

4. Environmental Sustainability and Conservation: Ferguson is a vocal supporter of environmental sustainability and conservation, drawing attention to issues including animal welfare, climate change, and deforestation. Through her work with organizations like Greenpeace and the WWF, Ferguson inspires others to take action to address environmental concerns by endorsing policies and legislation that protect the environment for future generations.

5. Social Justice and Equity: Ferguson uses her platform to advocate for social justice and equity while speaking out against racism, prejudice, and injustice in all of its

manifestations. Ferguson works with organizations like Human Rights Watch and the ACLU to elevate the voices of oppressed people and promote empathy, understanding, and unity in the fight for a more just and equitable society.

Rebecca Ferguson has had a profound and broad impact on social concerns, demonstrating her ardent wish to see positive change in the world. Ferguson serves as a potent reminder of the importance of using one's platform for social good and motivating positive change in the world, whether she is advocating for women's rights, fighting for the rights of immigrants, raising awareness of mental health concerns, or speaking out against injustice.

CHAPTER 6: AWARDS AND RECOMMENDATIONS:

Rebecca Ferguson has won numerous awards and acclaim for her acting prowess both domestically and internationally during the course of her career. The following is a comprehensive summary of some of the honors and prizes she has received:

1. Guldbagge Awards: Ferguson has won multiple Guldbagge Awards, the most coveted honors for Swedish film. She won the Best Actress Guldbagge Award in 2011 for her performance in the film "Miss Kicki." Her parts in other Swedish films, like "En Kongelig Affaere" (2012) and "Vi" (2013), have also earned her nominations.

2. Critics' Choice Movie Awards: Ferguson received high appreciation and admiration for her performance as Ilsa Faust in "Mission: Impossible – Rogue Nation" (2015). She was nominated for the Critics' Choice Movie Award for Best Actress in an Action Film for her riveting portrayal of the enigmatic MI6 agent.

3. Empire Awards: Ferguson's breakout performance in "Mission: Impossible – Rogue Nation" earned her a nomination for the 2016 Empire Award for Best Female

Newcomer. Her performance of Ilsa Faust was well received by critics and spectators alike, solidifying her status as an action heroine worth seeing.

4. Saturn Awards: Ferguson's talents in the science fiction and action genres have earned him accolades for the Saturn Awards. She was nominated in 2016 for a Saturn Award for Best Supporting Actress for her role in "Mission: Impossible – Rogue Nation," showcasing her versatility as an actress.

5. Screen Actors Guild Awards: Ferguson's outstanding performances in films and television have earned her a nomination for the Screen Actors Guild Awards. Due to the favorable reviews and enduring impact of her depiction of Serena Joy Waterford in "The Handmaid's Tale," she received a nomination for the Screen Actors Guild Award in 2018 for Outstanding Performance by an Ensemble in a Dramatic Series.

6. Other Recognition: In addition to official honors and nominations, Ferguson's skills and services to the entertainment sector have been recognized by a range of media sources, reviewers, and industry professionals. She has been featured on lists of talented actresses, upcoming performers, and well-known celebrities, cementing her status as one of Hollywood's most compelling actresses.

Rebecca Ferguson's recognition and honors demonstrate her exceptional talent, versatility, and impact on the motion picture and television industries. Ferguson's numerous honors, which include nominations from esteemed worldwide organizations and important awards in Sweden, attest to the public's appreciation and recognition of her compelling performances and artistic accomplishments.

6.1 Major Award Nominations:

Because of her outstanding talent and engaging performances, Rebecca Ferguson has received countless major award nominations over her career. Despite her recognition on a national and international level, the following offers a detailed analysis of some of the noteworthy awards for which she has received nominations:

1. Critics' Choice Movie Awards: Ferguson was nominated for Best Actress in an Action Film for her role as Ilsa Faust in "Mission: Impossible – Rogue Nation" (2015). Her portrayal of the enigmatic MI6 agent garnered her praise from both the public and critics, solidifying her status as an action heroine to watch.

2. Empire Awards: Ferguson was nominated in 2016 for the Empire Award for Best Female Newcomer in light of her outstanding performance in "Mission: Impossible – Rogue Nation." Her compelling portrayal of Ilsa Faust, which garnered praise for its depth, subtlety, and all-around badassness, cemented her place as a rising star in the action genre.

3. Saturn Awards: Ferguson's talents in the science fiction and action genres have earned him accolades for the Saturn Awards. She was nominated in 2016 for a Saturn Award for Best Supporting Performer for her role in "Mission: Impossible – Rogue Nation," showcasing her versatility and impact as a genre-bending performer.

4. Screen Actors Guild Awards: Ferguson's outstanding performances in films and television have earned her a nomination for the Screen Actors Guild Awards. With her work in "The Handmaid's Tale," she was nominated in 2018 for the Screen Actors Guild Award for Outstanding Performance by an Ensemble in a Drama Series, demonstrating her ability to fascinate audiences on both large and small screens.

5. Golden Globe Awards: Ferguson hasn't had a Golden Globe nomination yet, although both fans and reviewers have commended her performances in highly regarded films and television shows. As her career develops, she remains a formidable contender to win awards from prestigious organizations like the Hollywood Foreign Press Association.

6. Academy Awards (Oscars): Ferguson hasn't been nominated for an Academy Award yet, but her skill, adaptability, and commitment to her work make her a serious prospect for future recognition from the

Academy. If she continues to give compelling performances in a range of roles and genres, she will undoubtedly make her imprint on the greatest Hollywood stage.

Rebecca Ferguson's major award nominations are evidence of the public regard and recognition she has gained for her ability, versatility, and impact in the motion picture and television industries. Her continued successes and recognition, even though she hasn't yet won a trophy from these prestigious events, are evidence of her exceptional talent and her popularity as an actress.

6.2 Victories and Conquests:

Throughout her career, Rebecca Ferguson has experienced significant success on the home and international stages. Both critics and viewers have praised her for her skill, adaptability, and commitment to her craft. Here's a thorough look at some of her biggest victories and accomplishments:

1. Guldbagge Awards: Ferguson has won multiple Guldbagge Awards, which are the most prized accolades in Swedish cinema. She was honored with the 2011 Guldbagge Award for Best Actress for her role in the movie "Miss Kicki." Her performance of the major part won her multiple honors, establishing her as one of Sweden's leading actresses.

2. Critics' Choice Movie Awards: Ferguson was nominated for Best Actress in an Action Picture, a category that includes her role as Ilsa Faust in "Mission: Impossible – Rogue Nation" (2015). Even though she did not win the prize, her nomination showed the value of her performance and female capacity to compete in the action genre, which is dominated by men.

3. Other Awards and Nominations: In addition to her wins and nominations at important award ceremonies, Ferguson's talent and contributions to the entertainment business have been recognized by a range of media sources, reviewers, and industry insiders. She has been featured on lists of talented actresses, upcoming performers, and well-known celebrities, cementing her status as one of Hollywood's most compelling actresses.

4. Box Office Success: Ferguson is a financially successful star of multiple box office hits, including "Mission: Impossible" and "The Greatest Showman," which have brought in billions of dollars from ticket sales worldwide. Her parts in these popular films have contributed to her becoming a bankable celebrity and a priceless asset to any project.

5. Critical Acclaim: Throughout her career, Ferguson has received praise for her genuineness, versatility, and ability to fully and nuancedly inhabit a range of roles. Reviews that have commended her performances for their emotional relevance, complexity, and all-around compelling presence on film have helped her become known as one of the most gifted and varied actors of her generation.

6. Global attention and Acclaim: Ferguson's success in Hollywood has earned her attention and admiration on a

global level, expanding her fan base and solidifying her status as a Hollywood icon. Her performances have connected with audiences all around the world, winning her a passionate following and securing her place as a significant figure in the entertainment industry.

Rebecca Ferguson's achievements demonstrate her exceptional skill, versatility, and impact on the film business. Ferguson's professional journey shows her dedication to her work and her ability to captivate audiences with her talent, charisma, and sincerity. It starts with her well-received parts in Swedish films and concludes with her success in blockbusters in Hollywood.

6.3 Highlights of the Acceptance Speech:

Since Rebecca Ferguson has maintained a low profile in the public eye, information on specific acceptance speeches she may have made at award ceremonies or other events is limited. Nevertheless, I can offer you a basic notion of what her acceptance speech highlights might include, drawing upon recurrent themes and emotions expressed by performers in similar situations:

1. Gratitude: Like many performers, Ferguson would undoubtedly express her gratitude to those who supported and guided her during her career. This could include family, friends, mentors, and other members of the cast and crew, as well as fans who have continuously shown their support and thanks for her work.

2. Recognition: Ferguson may acknowledge the significance of the award or distinction she is receiving while simultaneously expressing humility and thanks for being recognized by her peers. She might think about the importance of the project or effort for which she is getting acknowledged, as well as how it has affected her personal and professional lives.

3. Inspiration: Ferguson might talk about the concepts and techniques that motivate her acting and offer an

understanding of her artistic approach. She might pay tribute to the characters she has portrayed and the stories she has been privileged to bring to life, highlighting the importance of media representation and the storytelling's capacity to alter.

4. Social Commentary: Given her commitment to social issues and advocacy work, Ferguson can utilize her platform to raise awareness of important causes and subjects that are close to her heart. She might seize the opportunity to raise awareness of matters such as women's rights, mental health awareness, refugee help, and environmental preservation, encouraging others to join her in making a difference in the world.

5. Last Words of Hope and Encouragement: Ferguson may close by urging others to follow their passions, embrace who they are, and stand up for what they believe to be right. She can emphasize the need of having courage, empathy, and resilience in the face of adversity, encouraging others to find strength and support in their relationships and communities. Though the exact details might vary depending on the circumstance and event, Rebecca Ferguson's acceptance speeches would likely highlight her genuine humility, love of her job, and commitment to leveraging her position for positive change overall.

CHAPTER 7: CONSEQUENCES AND ENDOWMENT:

Rebecca Ferguson's career and influence in the entertainment industry are defined by her outstanding talent, versatility, and dedication to her profession. Even though she is only in the early stages of her career, her contributions to film and television have already had a significant impact on both industry insiders and spectators. This is a detailed analysis of her legacy and impact:

1. Actress's Versatility: Ferguson's ability to portray a variety of roles with depth, realism, and sensitivity has won her praise and affection from critics and audiences alike. She has proven her flexibility as an actor by enthralling viewers in everything from action thrillers to period dramas with her compelling performances and magnetic presence on screen.

2. Diversity and Representation: The importance of diversity and representation in the entertainment industry is demonstrated by Ferguson's position as a Swedish-English woman in Hollywood. Her ability to get significant roles in highly regarded television series

and movie franchises is proof of the growing need for different voices and viewpoints in mainstream media.

3. Breaking Stereotypes: Ferguson has pushed the limits of traditional gender roles in television and movies by showcasing strong, complex female characters. Whether she's playing a cunning spy, a fearless action heroine, or a complex historical figure, Ferguson brings nuance and realness to every part. This encourages viewers to question stereotypes of power and femininity.

4. Advocacy and Social Impact: The idea that Ferguson is more than just an actor has been reinforced by her commitment to social causes and her participation in advocacy activities. Through her work with charitable organizations, public awareness campaigns, and philanthropic efforts, she has used her platform to raise awareness of important problems like refugee help, mental health awareness, women's rights, and environmental conservation.

5. encouragement for Future Generations: Ferguson's success story serves as an encouragement to aspiring actors and artists across the globe. Her ascent from humble origins to international renown is evidence that one may succeed in life by using talent, perseverance, and hard work. Through sharing her experiences and knowledge, Ferguson inspires others to embrace their

uniqueness, pursue their passions, and make a good difference in their communities and beyond.

 Rebecca Ferguson's legacy and influence in the entertainment industry are defined by her tremendous skill, her commitment to her craft, and her determination to use her platform for positive change. Ferguson's influence transcends Hollywood and has a profound effect on people's hearts and minds everywhere, whether she is inspiring viewers with her alluring on-screen personas or advocating for important social problems off-screen.

7.1 Impacting the Amusement Industry:

Beyond her compelling on-screen personas, Rebecca Ferguson has had a huge impact on the entertainment business. Her lobbying work, talent, and flexibility have greatly impacted many areas of the company. This is a detailed examination of her influence:

1. Versatility and Range: People's perceptions of what it means to be a starring actress have altered as a result of Ferguson's ability to play a variety of roles and transition across genres with ease. Her willingness to take on demanding parts in films and television has inspired other performers to explore new creative frontiers and push the boundaries of their profession.

2. Diversity and Representation: As a woman of Swedish and English ancestry, Ferguson's presence in Hollywood has helped to enhance both of these factors in the entertainment industry. Her ability to land major roles in highly regarded television series and expensive film franchises has inspired individuals to embrace their own cultural identity and heritage and raised awareness of the need for a diversity of perspectives in mainstream media.

3. Empowerment of Women: By presenting strong, nuanced female characters, Ferguson has increased the influence that women have both on and off-screen. With the depth and complexity she has brought to her characters, she has challenged established gender norms and stereotypes, paving the way for more nuanced and authentic representations of women in film and television. Her characters serve as role models for women worldwide and aspiring actors, encouraging them to embrace their individuality, tenacity, and strength.

4. Social Cause Advocacy: Ferguson's commitment to social concerns and her advocacy activities have mobilized her followers and colleagues to take action and raise awareness of important topics. By using her platform to speak out on causes like women's rights, refugee help, mental health awareness, and environmental protection, she has inspired change and rallied support in communities all over the world.

5. International Appeal: As a result of Ferguson's global success, Swedish film has gained greater recognition across the globe and Scandinavian performers are now more well-liked elsewhere. Her collaborations with renowned directors and actors from many backgrounds have fostered more intercultural communication and

collaboration in the industry, opening up more opportunities for international talent to shine.

6. Inspiration for Future Generations: Ferguson's journey from relative obscurity to international success serves as an inspiration to aspiring actors and artists everywhere. Her sincerity, tenacity, and bravery in the face of adversity serve as examples of how skill, hard work, and dedication may lead one to achieve their goals. Ferguson shares her experiences and knowledge to inspire others to embrace their uniqueness, follow their ambitions, and make a lasting impression on the entertainment world.

Rebecca Ferguson's skill, versatility, advocacy work, and appeal to a global audience have all contributed to her wide-ranging influence on the entertainment business. As she raises awareness of social concerns and enthralls audiences with her performances, her influence on business and society at large is certain to grow. She will surely affect the future of narrative in motion pictures and television shows and promote positive change.

7.2 Cultural Significance:

Rebecca Ferguson is a culturally significant figure in the entertainment industry for several reasons that relate to broader societal shifts and beliefs. This is an in-depth examination of her cultural relevance:

1. Diversity and Representation: Ferguson's Swedish and English origin and background contribute to the range of representation that is shown on film. Ferguson's presence, which reflects the wide tapestry of cultures and identities in today's global society, signifies a step towards more diversity in an industry that has hitherto been dominated by a restricted range of origins and races.

2. Empowerment of Women: By presenting strong, nuanced female characters, Ferguson subverts gender norms and stereotypes, empowering women. Her characters consistently exhibit agency, intelligence, and resilience; they portray women as strong, multifaceted individuals with distinct histories to share and objectives to work for. This portrayal resonates with audiences seeking more complex depictions of women in the media.

3. Breaking Boundaries: Ferguson's versatility as an actress is seen in her ability to play a variety of roles and transition between different genres. Her adaptability allows her to play a wider variety of parts and challenges the way performers are traditionally categorized, shattering stereotypes and encouraging a casting and storytelling process that is more inclusive and flexible.

4. Cultural Exchange: As a well-known actress worldwide, Ferguson encourages cultural exchanges across countries and regions. Her collaborations with performers and filmmakers from different origins foster mutual understanding and communication beyond cultural barriers, forging connections and shared experiences that transcend national boundaries.

5. Social Advocacy: Ferguson encourages people to take up social causes such as women's rights, environmental preservation, refugee help, and mental health awareness by bringing important concerns to people's attention. She uses her position to raise awareness of these concerns and mobilize support, serving as an example of the ability of celebrities to ignite social movements and effect positive change.

6. Inspiration and Aspiration: Ferguson's ascent from relative obscurity to broad acclaim serves as an example for aspiring actors and artists globally. Her perseverance,

dedication, and sincerity serve as an inspiration to others pursuing their goals and breaking into the entertainment industry, fostering a climate of ambition, creativity, and self-expression.

Rebecca Ferguson's cultural relevance extends beyond her particular acting achievements to encompass broader issues of social advocacy, diversity, empowerment, and inclusivity. As long as she continues to wow crowds with her performances and advocates for causes close to her heart, she will continue to have a significant impact on culture and society. She will also catalyze change and advance the entertainment sector's ongoing development.

7.3 Upcoming Initiatives and Projects:

1. Film Projects: Given her track record of success in indie and mainstream blockbusters, Ferguson is likely to continue exploring a range of film projects. This could be leading roles in well-known franchises, directing collaborations on high-profile dramas, or opportunities to work on side projects that allow her to venture into uncharted artistic territory.

2. Television Ventures: Given the increasing popularity and significance of television series, particularly in light of the rise of streaming services, Ferguson may investigate prospects in the television business. Whether Ferguson is starring in limited series, anthology dramas, or original projects for streaming services, television offers a rich environment for narrative and character development that would appeal to his creative sensibilities.

3. International Collaborations: Ferguson may seek out opportunities to collaborate globally to work with directors and actors from other cultural backgrounds, given her widespread fame. Co-productions, foreign-language movies, or multinational ensemble casts can provide Ferguson the chance to push her

artistic boundaries and explore uncharted creative territory.

4. Producer and Directorial Ventures: Ferguson may investigate opportunities to assume additional producing or directing responsibilities behind the camera as her career progresses. If Ferguson took on more creative control and participated in the planning and execution of projects, she might further showcase her aesthetic vision and contribute to the industry's growth of captivating stories and storytelling.

5. Advocacy and Philanthropy: Ferguson's commitment to social problems and philanthropy will undoubtedly continue to be a big part of her future endeavors. Ferguson's dedication to bringing about a positive change in the world will persistently inform her choices and deeds, whether she is spearheading her charitable projects, utilizing her position to raise awareness of important issues, or providing support to groups and initiatives through her advocacy work.

6. Personal Growth and Exploration: Ferguson may prioritize both her professional and personal growth and exploration in her future undertakings. This might be making time for self-reflection, engaging in hobbies

unrelated to acting, or seeking out new challenges and chances to advance her career and personal growth.

Her commitment to artistic brilliance, personal fulfillment, and social activism will undoubtedly affect her future decisions and aspirations. Audiences will undoubtedly be inspired and captivated by her talent, sincerity, and love of storytelling as she continues to grow as an actor, activist, and creative force in the entertainment industry.

CONCLUSION

Rebecca Ferguson's career in the entertainment industry has been shaped by her extraordinary skill, versatility, and commitment to making a good impact both on and off-screen. From her early beginnings in Swedish cinema to her widespread acclaim as a Hollywood star, Ferguson has captivated audiences with her captivating performances, empowered women with her portrayal of strong, complex characters, and raised awareness about important social issues through her advocacy work.

Throughout her career, Ferguson's influence has extended beyond the performing arts, impacting perceptions, inspiring change, and promoting greater inclusivity, diversity, and representation in the entertainment industry. Her dedication to her work, her sincerity, and her courage to follow their ambitions, accept their uniqueness, and make a lasting impact on the world serve as an inspiration to aspiring actors and artists worldwide.

Ferguson will continue to have an impact on story, representation, and social change in the future both inside and outside of the entertainment industry as she advances as an actor, activist, and cultural icon. Whether she's captivating audiences with her on-screen personas, advocating for important causes, or inspiring others to pursue their dreams, Ferguson will continue to have an impact for many years to come, leaving a lasting impression on people's hearts and minds everywhere.

Manufactured by Amazon.ca
Bolton, ON

42470061R00048